Annapolis Visit

A PHOTOGRAPHIC ESSAY

ON MARYLAND'S

ANCIENT CITY

TEXT & PHOTOGRAPHS

BY

Mary Mitchell

FOREWORD

BY JAMES BIDDLE

Barre Publishers, Barre, Massachusetts 1969

FRONTISPIECE:
Looking up Cornhill Street to the State House

Half the royalties received by the author
from the publication of this book will be
contributed to Historic Annapolis, Inc.

EVERYONE has a love affair with Annapolis, as one of the aficionados has said, and this goes back into the earliest history of America's only colonial capital (1694) which still serves today as a state capital. Through the discerning camera of Mary Mitchell, we now have an enchanting memory book of a city which combines a proud heritage with a hurly-burly present.

One of its early and perceptive visitors was the young Thomas Jefferson who wrote his college classmate John Page at William and Mary on May 25, 1766, from Annapolis: "The situation of this place is extremely beautiful, and very commodious for trade . . . . The houses in general are better than those in Williamsburg, but the gardens more indifferent . . . ." Apparently Mr. William Paca's great house had been completed but his handsome pleasure gardens, currently being restored, were still being developed.

Mrs. Mitchell's camera has caught the beauty which still remains as recorded in letters of early travelers; "The courthouse, situated on an eminence at the back of the town, commands a variety of views highly interesting; the entrance of the Severn, the majestic Chesapeak, and the eastern shore of Maryland, being all united in one resplendent assemblage. Vessels of various sizes and figures are continually floating before the eye; which, while they add to the beauty of the scene, excite ideas of the most pleasing nature." Beyond that she has seen and recorded the problems of a city of great historic and architectural significance trying desperately to assure the presence of its past in an era when the Naval Academy is literally straining at its seams, the boating interests have revitalized its old harbor but in doing so are swallowing up and destroying choice historic bayside properties, and a business community has not entirely realized its greatest potential asset—its architectural heritage.

Here is one of today's dichotomies, and let us hope this sensitive record of it will do much to reconcile the magnificent past of Annapolis with a more considerate future.

JAMES BIDDLE, *President*
National Trust for Historic Preservation

ACKNOWLEDGEMENTS

EVER SINCE James Stoddert drew his famous map in 1718, Annapolis has been pictured by many artists, novelists, cartographers, historians, journalists, poets, and even other photographers. So it is with some humility that I add to this list of publications still another attempt to record its unique charm and heritage. If there is here anything fresh in point-of-view or content, and if I, too, succeed, it is due largely to the contributions in time and interest of many proud citizens who were eager to see their favorite town presented in as full, happy and accurate a way as possible.

In particular I want to thank Mr. and Mrs. Stanley S. Wohl, gracious owners of the Brice House, who opened it to my camera, and shared their library and profound knowledge of local history and architecture; L. Harvey Poe, Jr., owner of the Carroll Settler house on Market Street, who was equally hospitable; Vernon D. Tate, former Librarian and now Archivist of the United States Naval Academy, whose suggestions on Academy lore helped me substantially in building up that section; James Burch, Member, A. I. A., whose willingness to comment on the Ridout House I appreciated; Lina Beth Hallock and her dog Queenie who ran down the Weems path as I set up for a photograph; John Hebden of Fawcett Boat Supplies who kindly assembled the window of old nautical instruments; the Maryland Inn who never failed to find me a room; Mrs. Norma Dale, Historic Annapolis Guide; Dr. and Mrs. Henry H. Balch, owners of *Innisfree* from whose deck several key photographs were taken; Mrs. A. St. Clair Wright who suggested many photographs as well as gave when asked much helpful advice, and proofread the final caption-copy; and Orlando Gault, Duane Mansley and their crew for whose competence and cooperation as the book shaped up, I was ever grateful.

The captions are based on information culled for the most part from the following bibliography. They have been checked carefully, and it is hoped that no errors mar the final copy. If so the fault is mine and mine alone.

TABLE OF CONTENTS

CHURCH CIRCLE

HISTORICALLY, the proper access to Annapolis would be via Spa Creek and the inner harbor, for this is how the water-minded Tobacco Society of the Colonial Era entered its capital. But today most visitors take the Scenic Route along Northwest Street or drive in along West to Church Circle. Since this is the heart of the Old Town, we shall begin right here. The photograph was taken about a block inside a hypothetical line representing the original moat and palisade enclosing the town. Beyond was wilderness.

This approach also serves to emphasize the reason why Annapolis became the provincial capital, a sequence of history one should understand before entering the Ancient City, as the Continental Congress called Annapolis. In 1632 Charles I granted the second Lord Baltimore, Cecilius Calvert, who was a Roman Catholic, a charter for a province to be carved from land north of Virginia. He called it "Terra Mariae" after Charles' wife Henrietta Maria, and planned a colony where religious freedom would prevail.

But tumultuous events in England reduced this beauteous dream to ashes. In 1688 Protestant William and Mary replaced Catholic James II, and the Baltimores lost their rich colony to the Crown. (Twenty-seven years later it was restored to the fourth Lord Baltimore who publicly renounced his Catholic faith, became a Protestant, and had a Protestant son.) The first royal governor removed the capital in 1694 from St. Mary's on the Patuxent to Annarundell towne where Protestants sympathetic to the Crown had settled around a convenient harbor, and the new town was named for Queen Mary's sister, Princess Anne, who in 1702 succeeded as Queen Anne.

The first St. Anne's Church was erected in 1704 on the lower of two circles which the City Fathers and the Royal Governor planned on the east-west axis. By 1775 a new building was needed, and the old one torn down. But the Revolutionary War intervened, and timber and brick secured for the second church were confiscated for war use. In 1792 a second St. Anne's was built on the Circle with two steeples and cupolas. This in turn disappeared in 1858 by fire. The present church was erected the next year, incorporating the old walls in the new.

Church Circle—approach from West Street

Old Church Yard

IN THE COLONIAL ERA Annapolis developed like an English village with its church at the town's heart and its quality buried in the Old Church Yard, their number growing with the decades. Soon the Yard was full, and when the present postoffice was built across the Circle, the cemetery was moved north along Northwest Street. Some of the oldest and richest worthies were allowed to remain, and even a noble English Tory, the last Colonial governor, Sir Robert Eden. He left Annapolis when the Revolution began, but loved it so much he returned afterwards to die and be buried here.

The tomb of Sir Robert Eden is in the foreground

The Reynolds Tavern

THIS GAMBREL-ROOFED BUILDING erected in 1735, now the administrative offices of the Annapolis and Anne Arundel County Public Library, had a lusty beginning as a tavern. William Reynolds, its keeper who also made gentlemen's hats of softest beaver, must have prospered.

Nearby out West Street, beyond the palisade, ran the racetrack. Importing English and Arabian stallions to improve the small local breed, the English governor, Sir Samuel Ogle, and the wealthy Annapolitan, Benjamin Tasker, were enthusiastic turfmen. During Raceweek aficionados from all over the Colonies, including George Washington, were frequent visitors at the track and the tavern. Perhaps the founding of the Maryland Jockey Club, known to have taken place in Annapolis in 1743, was consummated here.

During the Revolution and the War of 1812 war surged all around Annapolis but the actual fighting never touched it. However with its central location on the Bay, with its many attractions such as racing, theatre, balls, and shopping, Annapolis was a constant place of assembly for public events and conferences. It was also the Revolutionary supply depot from which the army in Virginia was outfitted. Lafayette, Rochambeau and many other Frenchmen assembled here in 1781 before joining the American armies. In short, hostelries were indispensable and this is the most imposing of the many that survive.

THE SHIELD on the caps of Annapolis Police officers represents the Reverse of the Great Seal of Maryland, brought over in the early days of the Colony. It consists of an escutcheon bearing the Calvert and Crossland arms quartered. Crossland was the family of the first Lord Baltimore's mother. Above is an earl's coronet. The shield is supported on one side by a farmer and on the other by a fisherman, symbolizing Lord Baltimore's two estates of Maryland and Avalon in Newfoundland.

The State of Maryland seal on the police officer's cap

SCHOOL STREET winds up toward State Circle. At its head once stood King William's School, Maryland's first public school, established in 1694.

Looking from Church Circle up School Street

Government House

ALONG THE WAY you pass Government House, photographed here on May Day when this charming town blooms with traditional bouquets on doorstep, shutters or gate. The governor's mansion was built in 1866, but was remodeled in 1936 into a Georgian structure. The building and its gardens occupy a five-sided block.

STATE CIRCLE
TO THE
HALL OF RECORDS

The MARYLAND STATE HOUSE is the oldest capitol building in the Nation still fulfilling its original legislative purpose. Begun in 1695, the first little Capitol was plagued with disaster. Archives were lost because careless workmen left them open to gusty weather. The contractor died, sober workmen were hard to find, it was struck by lightning in 1704 and burned with a total loss of records.

The next building was taller and bigger with a more elaborate cupola. The Circle is 538 feet across and, during this period of the fast expanding colony, the Circle grew crowded with smaller structures intended to supplement the Capitol itself. By 1770 eight buildings clustered around it on the open parklike area where today people rendezvous and enjoy pleasant sunny benches. These buildings were a Public Necessary, King William's School, the Armory or Conference Chamber where balls and receptions were held, a Re-pository for Old Records, the Powder House or Magazine, a Market House, and the Treasury which now is the only one left.

By 1766 this structure was so run down that Thomas Jefferson wrote from Annapolis in May of that year that "the old courthouse, judging from its form and appearance, was built in the year one . ." The pride of a Virginian in the Williamsburg courthouse may have prompted this comment. In any case it was decided in 1769 to tear down the Capitol and rebuild. The present building was completed between 1772 and 1780.

In this picture though, there is one prominent Annapolis feature which its ardent preservationists can do without, namely, the obsolete utility poles, transformers and wires which clutter and festoon every street and vista in town. The power companies agree they ought to be put underground, but so far, at any rate, "Mañana" seems to be the only answer.

The State House

JOHN BARON DE KALB, 1721-1780, played an unsung hero's role in the American Revolution. Born in Bayreuth, Germany, he joined the French Army at 21, and meeting Benjamin Franklin in Paris, was inspired to join the Revolutionary cause. He persuaded Lafayette to support it too and both came in 1777 to America. General De Kalb commanded the Second Maryland Brigade in the Battle of Camden, fought in the swamps of South Carolina, August 16, 1780. Pierced by eleven wounds he died fighting. The United States Congress voted then to erect a monument to him in Maryland. But it was not unveiled until the 106th anniversary of his death. Ephraim Keyser was the sculptor. The statue stands where scholars believe King William's School was.

The De Kalb Statue

*Looking up Chancery Lane
to the State House*

CHANCERY LANE connects Main Street and State Circle, and is typical of many alleys and shortcuts crisscrossing the irregular "parcels" or blocks that resulted when streets were designed to radiate from not only one but two circles and along the compass points. The supe-riority of temporal over spiritual authority may have satisfied the City Fathers. But the result today means headaches for title-searchers and historians who want to document a single building on an odd-shaped lot with perhaps ten other buildings set down helter-skelter on it.

A CAPITOL GUARD takes down the Maryland State flag at sunset every day. It bears the handsome yellow and black Calvert colors. The crosses for the Crossland family are red and white.

CHIEF JUSTICE of the United States Supreme Court from 1836 until he died in 1864, Roger B. Taney broods in bronze outside the State House portico. Having studied law in Annapolis and first practiced here, he would have been proud to see himself so honored. Aware of the many distinguished Colonial and patriot lawyers at the Annapolis bar, he called the town the "Athens" of America.

LIKE A SANCTUARY in the midst of the otherwise busy State House, the celebrated Old Senate Chamber saw George Washington resign his commission as Commander-in-Chief of the United States Army, December 23, 1783. General Thomas Mifflin, president of the Continental Congress, sat in the chair on the dais, and Washington stood by the table on the near side.

The Old Senate Chamber

The John Trumbull painting

TWO ARTISTS painted this historic scene, Edwin White whose painting hangs on the stairway wall of the State House, and John Trumbull whose painting hangs in the rotunda of the United States Capitol in Washington. The latter was chosen to illustrate the scene because not only are the colors brighter but the architectural background of the Chamber is clearer and more inclusive. It is believed that William Buckland, the English joiner who was working in Annapolis in the 1770s, carved the tobacco-leaf moldings and the cornices.

However both artists neglected their homework, as Maryland's former Governor Theodore R. McKeldin eloquently described in his article "Hats On For General Washington" in *American Heritage*, August, 1956. The members of Congress present sat with hats on by prearranged plan. In 1783 the Continental Congress was without prestige. The Constitution had not been written; it had no authority. Plagued by a general indiffer-

ence, it mustered only eighteen men for this session, representing seven states out of thirteen.

By contrast George Washington was the popular hero. When he arrived in Annapolis, December 20, he wrote the Congress asking permission to resign and, with his usual punctilio, requested that he be notified how the Congress wished to receive his resignation. A committee established the protocol. This stated that until the resignation was finished, the members would keep their hats on. *He* was to bow to *them,* while they remained seated and would acknowledge his obeisances only by briefly tipping their hats.

At the appointed hour of noon, he entered the Chamber, and at every point in his address conformed to the instructions. When he drew out from his bosom his commission and placed the document in Mifflin's hands, his memories overcame him and tears ran down his cheeks. Then he bowed and the Congress at last uncovered.

LOOKING DOWN from the balcony in the House of Delegates. When this photograph was taken, the Maryland Constitutional Convention was being held in the fall of 1967. H. Vernon Eney, Chairman, opens a daily plenary session.

The Senate Chamber across the hall resembles that of the House, and both constitute the Annex added to the Capitol in 1902-1905. The Senate is in red leather, the House in blue.

BUILT AROUND 1720 this gambrel-roofed house on the Circle, owned by the State, was once the home of Cornelius Brooksby and later of John Shaw, the cabinetmaker, in the Golden Era of Annapolis, 1765-1775. Shaw made the original furniture for the Senate Chamber, but most of it has either disappeared or been located elsewhere. The desk and chair, however, on the dais are original.

The Brooksby-Shaw House

Two BOYS examine a plaque on a cannon brought by
the first colonists at St. Mary's in 1634. The cupola of
the Calvary Methodist Church is in the background.

Tecumseh

orated. To preserve this venerable Being, the Class of 1891 had Tecumseh cast in bronze and placed here in June, 1930.

Soon after, his sphere of patronage was extended to encompass the whole Navy in its annual contest with Army. Every year now, just before the big game, students apply his warpaint in Navy colors, yellow and blue, hoping his favor will grant them a victory.

The Naval Museum

THE RANGE of the Museum's memorabilia is outstanding. Stephen Decatur's christening cap contrasts with the saddle complete with fur trappings of Admiral William F. Halsey. In one case is a collection of class rings from 1869 to present, while in another is a rime-encrusted porthole recovered from the *USS Maine*. Here you have a statue of Joan of Arc presented by the people of Brest to the American Navy 4 July 1918; in the middle are daggers, beheading swords, and poniards from foreign countries. To the left is the ship *Niger*, an American whaler of 1865. The Naval Museum's ship-model collection numbers well over four hundred.

A door knocker on Mahan Hall

Bancroft Hall from the harbor

THIS SPRAWLING MASS of French Renaissance granite, housing the full brigade of four thousand midshipmen, is named for the Yankee who established the Naval Academy at Annapolis. Born in Worcester, Massachusetts, in 1800, and a distinguished American historian, George Bancroft entered the cabinet of President James K. Polk as Secretary of the Navy in 1845.

At that time the Army owned a derelict fort at Annapolis built in 1808 when the capital was still considered a place of military importance. Located at the junction of the River Severn with the harbor, Fort Severn offered ample water for stationing a vessel as a gun-

nery school, and in addition buildings for quartering men and for classrooms.

On August 15, 1845, the Fort was transferred from the Army to the Navy, and two months later school began. The transfer was executed in the summer without recourse to Congress. This would have endangered the whole plan by opening up the question to discussion and debate.

At the extreme right of the photograph is the East End of Bancroft Hall. There stood the octagonal-shaped Fort demolished in 1901 when construction began for the Academy's expansion after the Spanish-American War.

THE MEN form daily in the courtyard for lunch and before the Sunday Chapel service. Here they carry kneeling pads to protect their summer whites while in Chapel. On the morrow they will change to winter blues. The day before, Navy played Rice University of Texas in football. Unhappily, Navy was "fried".

THE CHAPEL'S LOFTY DOME is a prominent landmark on the Annapolis skyline.

64

THE RETREAT OF THE COLORS gives a heart-stirring finish to the Sunday service. Absolute silence prevails while the bearers elevate the Colors at the altar, turn and step briskly down into the nave. All remains silent as the pace accelerates so that the flags will billow out behind during the fast march to the end of the aisle where the Colors are then retired.

ON FAIR-WEATHER Wednesday afternoons spring and fall, the brigade parades on Worden Field. A dress rehearsal in March, however, when blustery winds can put the Colors askew, suggests the discipline bearers must maintain to execute the perfection of every parade.

In the background is Upshur Row occupied by Assistant Department Heads. The top brass who lived in the Row until 1900, when Porter Row was built, for them, called it "Oklahoma". They said pressure to get in resembled the land rush to Oklahoma.

Brigade rehearsal on Worden Field

Retreat of the Colors

Dahlgren Hall

DAHLGREN HALL is named for the naval ordnance expert of the Civil War, Admiral John Dahlgren. Now the Armory, it is the scene of many gala events like the Ring Dance during June Week. These pictures were taken on a March Sunday afternoon, called an "Agony After-noon", when plebes can enjoy an infrequent date. At any time one is apt to be asked by an upperclassman: "What's up?" And he *must* answer: "Fidelity's up on my bayonet-belt, Sir." "Fidelity" appears on the top of the buckle.

Interior of the Armory

A rack of bayonet-belts removed for the occasion

The Brice House from Gate Two

THE BRICE HOUSE
TO THE HARBOR

SET ON A TERRACE at East and Prince George Streets is a grand, five-section Colonial mansion, looking without and within much as it did during the American Revolution. Several factors are responsible for this happy circumstance. Limited to a small city area by a natural boundary of water on all sides but one, Annapolis was bypassed in the Nineteenth Century when the major canal and railroad lines were built. Her port facilities grew inadequate and her commercial shipping was lost as a sustaining resource. The prime source of their former wealth thus dissipated, owners of the great Georgian houses had no funds for "improvements", alterations and embellishments of the Victorian era. The old families lived, as one historian relates, like hermits.

Begun in the 1740s by John Brice II, a shipping merchant, this house was finished by his son Col. James Brice who inherited it in 1766. In 1769 he commissioned William Buckland to design and execute the interior joinery in the state rooms and reception hall, all in the elaborate manner of the period, "Golden Age" in Annapolis history.

Structurally and in its dimensions, the Brice House had no equal in Colonial America. The walls are three feet thick and so are the fieldstone crosses embedded therein. More than six feet thick, the endwall foundations support exceptionally broad gable chimneys which rise 90'6" from street-level to pinnacle, the tallest Georgian chimneys anywhere. Freestanding Georgian houses have two fronts: one facing the water approach, the other a garden. All bricks in the Brice House are oversize, and the walls of both fronts are featured by brickwork laid in the extravagant all-header bond, a method used exclusively in Eighteenth Century Annapolis.

Desiring to preserve the mansion in its original state and to use it as their home, the present owners bought the house from St. John's College which had utilized it as a faculty residence.

The ballroom in the Brice House

THE BALLROOM, and especially the mantel with its fine side-panels, is reminiscent of the Drawing-room in Marlborough House, London. Col. Brice married Juliana Jenings, a niece of Sarah Jenings Churchill, first Duchess of Marlborough.

COL. GEORGE WASHINGTON was often served from this dining room cupboard. In the Colonial Era the Governor's mansion, where he usually called, stood at one end of East Street with the State House at the other. The Brice house was midway between. Washington noted in his Diary and correspondence that he visited here often. Journeying to Annapolis some eighteen times before the War, he came to enjoy himself at the races, theatres, balls, and as a guest of the Tuesday Club to which James Brice, later Mayor of Annapolis, then belonged. Other records disclose that Generals Lafayette and Nathanael Greene, John Dickinson, and James Madison also visited here during the days of the early Republic.

The dining-room cupboard

THE GARDEN FRONT of the Brice House dwarfing a row of frame dwellings on Martin Street is seen through Gate Two of the Naval Academy.

The Brice House from East Street

HERE the quaint little house of Patrick Creagh with its single window and gambrel roof was built against its neighbor between 1735 and 1747. As he described himself in the records, Patrick Creagh was "painter, merchant, shipbuilder, farmer, mariner, contractor for the maintenance of His Majesty's forces, and ultimately, Gentleman."

Patrick Creagh's house

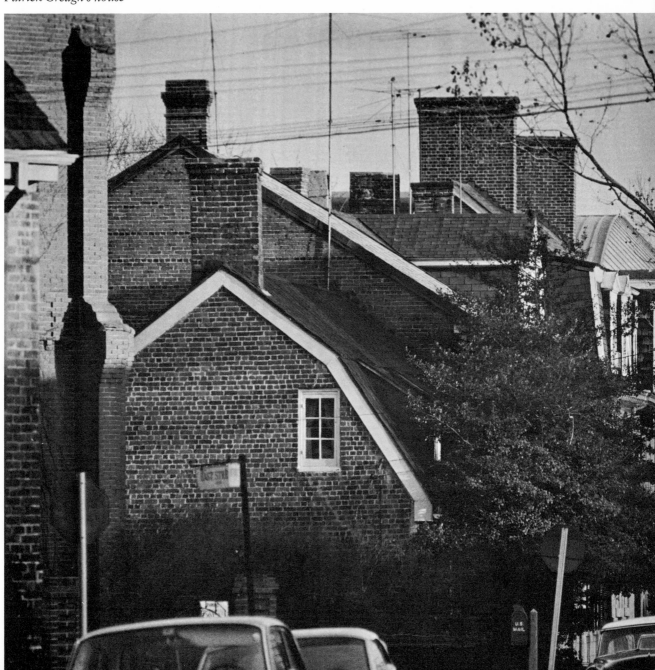

BEHIND STAGE before a performance of Eugene O'Neill's *Long Day's Journey Into Night* at the Colonial Theatre on East Street. The Colonial Players, an amateur group, has been active since 1948 in an historic tradition special to Annapolis. The first theatre in America was opened in Annapolis in 1752 by a London Troupe, and continued a long time.

A VIEW down Prince George in summer. This street was named for Prince George, later George II King of England. Prince George's County was named for Prince George of Denmark, husband of Queen Anne.

THESE VICTORIAN FACADES along Prince George
show restraint in deference to the more outstanding
Colonial architecture.

The Paca House

CROWDED NOW between buildings of other eras, Paca House was the town house of William Paca, patriot lawyer, Eastern Shore planter, and third governor of the State after the Revolution. Winston Churchill, author of *Richard Carvel*, the historical novel about the Revolutionary period set in Annapolis, had this house in mind as the residence of his heroine, Dorothy Manners. In Colonial days, the Paca Gardens extended to the water's edge at the corner of Martin Street and King George, and were the finest in Annapolis. Tree-shaded terraces swept down to a lake whose narrow end was spanned by a miniature Chinese Chippendale bridge.

Hitching-post on May Day

LOOKING DOWN Cornhill Street from State Circle at Christmas. Laid out and built up in the days of the sedan chair and the carriage, Cornhill has many pre-Revolutionary houses. Along with other old streets, its residents have battled the City Council to preserve the brick sidewalks.

Cornhill Street from State Circle

A barbershop where Cornhill and Fleet Streets intersect

A BARBERPOLE has marked this corner for a long time, Washington was traditionally shaved here before appearing before the Congress at noon on December 23, 1783. This wedge-shaped corner divides Fleet Street on the right and lower Cornhill on the left. Neither can be said to resemble its London namesake of the Eighteenth Century.

THE Slicer-Shiplap House, built in 1723 and documented in this year, is now the headquarters of Historic Annapolis, Inc., the non-profit organization which since 1952 has taken the lead in the preservation of authentic old Annapolis and of its attractive appearance as such. William Slicer was a cabinetmaker in the 1730s. Shiplap refers to the way the clapboard siding was applied.

The Slicer-Shiplap House at 18 Pinkney Street

The market place

THE OLD HARBOR

HERE IS A SECTION of today's dockspace and harbor. At left is the shedlike market built in 1858 to replace one erected in 1784, and the fifth market built in Annapolis. At right is Mandris' Restaurant, a Federal structure intact by 1824, which conceals under a brick facade and pitched roof two Georgian buildings set side by side. One was a house and the other Middleton's Tavern whose owner also ran a famous sailing ferry to the Eastern Shore. Bringing many noted figures like George Washington, Thomas Jefferson, and Benjamin Franklin to Annapolis, it helped to make the Maryland capital a popular port for Washington.

The relationship of these two buildings to the harbor suggests the pattern in which brick stores and shops, taverns and warehouses have looked out onto this scene for over two centuries. In all, thirty-two buildings, 72% of them built before 1840, combine to render the Annapolis dock space a unique survival of an early American port.

Originally the harbor reached to the Slicer-Shiplap House and, where parked cars are today, large vessels found wharfage beside docks piled with hogsheads and bales. Blockmakers, sailmakers, carpenters, ropewalks, and chandlers helped to mount expeditions or prepare ships for a sea voyage. Smaller vessels, snows, sloops, schooners and log canoes brought in produce from the interior to be exported, and toted the water-minded provincials into the capital for trading, church, visiting, court sessions, or any number of errands in the gay little city. They regarded it as much the kind of marine supply and merchandising center as in fact oystermen and yachtsmen do today.

AN HISTORIC ANNAPOLIS GUIDE meets boys from the freshman class of Cardinal Gibbons High School, Baltimore, on the City Dock to conduct them around the capital. Determined to tell the Annapolis story, the guides never grow discouraged by the kind of attention, or lack of it, they evoke from their audience, because, as this Navy wife explains, "We all have love affairs with Annapolis."

THIS Annapolis Port of Entry record for Lady Day 1748 is on file at the Hall of Records. Named for Annunciation Day, March 25, the phrase is still used in England to mean the day terminating the winter quarter.

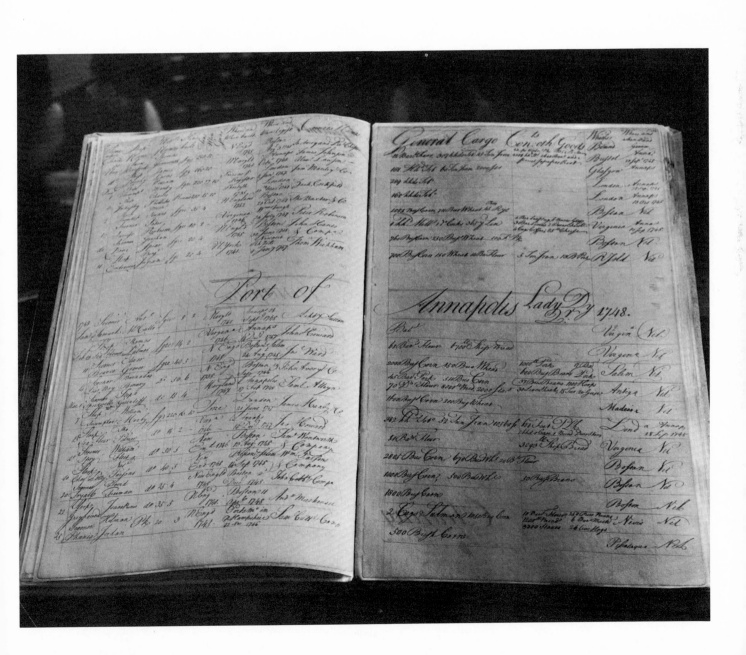

Old buildings on the "Ship Carpenter's" lot

86

THE BOWSPRITS and rigging of the oystermen's skip-jacks set against a background of old buildings recall the days of merchant sail. The building to the right is the traditional Colonial customs house. Annapolis was made a Port of Entry in 1683.

Bowsprits and old houses

The skipjack fleet

A FLEET of skipjacks, the Nation's last commercial sail, rocks gently at anchor in Annapolis harbor before setting out November 1 for oyster-dredging on Chesapeake Bay "rocks" or bars. Vanishing Americana, these stout singlemasted vessels are rigged astern with small powerboats which Maryland law permits owners to use as pushboats if the wind fails. Otherwise they must be hoisted inboard when over the "rocks", and dredging is then by windpower alone, except on Mondays and Tuesdays. With no more skipjacks being built, each year the number dwindles, only 45 remaining today of a fleet which numbered over two thousand fifty years ago.

Skipjack reflections on a golden October afternoon

THE *Thomas Clyde,* bows on. In the background is the Tecumseh, a condominium built in 1967 and an example of contemporary architecture, Annapolis-style.

SHIFTING OYSTERS from the *Howard* to the buy-boat *Mildred,* at the end of the City Dock.

THESE VESSELS, called patent tongers, are on the increase. Last year 139 were licensed in Anne Arundel County, many homebased in Annapolis. The law allows these vessels to use power to work their rigs. But unlike the skipjacks, they cannot use power dredges to dig the oyster. They use these tongs patented by a Crisfield, Maryland, inventor fifty years ago. Their season starts September 15, and both types must terminate March 31.

A "patent tonger"

The inner harbor on an early summer morning

A sloop on Spa Creek

ONE WOULD GIVE his bottom dollar for a sloop tied to his dock. The other couldn't care less.

On the horizon are five of the Navy's nine radio towers on Greenbury Point, another mariner's landmark.

HERE IS paraphernalia of the navigator, oldtime and used today, often found in old wills and inventories, and sold on Compromise Street in the only ship chandlery in Annapolis.

From left to right: miniature capstan; parallel rules; box of binoculars; pelorus with which to take bearings and sightings; antique globe; anchor light, class 3; belaying pin to secure halyards; stadimeter for taking bearings; brass megaphone made in Denmark; nylon sheets and leadlines; brass spinnaker socket.

Paraphernalia of the navigator

SPA CREEK TO BACK CREEK

THE ANNAPOLIS YACHT CLUB may recall the Tea-house of the August Moon, and indeed its style is called Japanese Modern. But its origins are one hundred percent local. In 1886 the Severn Boat Club was organized and rented a portion of the waterfront from St. Mary's Church that was said to have been the site of a trading post operated by one Proctor in the seventeenth century. A one-story frame building was erected which grew like Topsy with porches, a second story and a ball-room. For almost eighty years this sufficed until the present clubhouse was built and opened in 1963.

The Annapolis Yacht Club

MOST RACING takes place further out in the Bay.
But in summer, on Wednesdays, an all-class series starts
at 6.30 P.M. from near the Naval Academy's seawall
and finishes about sunset at the Yacht Club.

The DRAWBRIDGE to Eastport replaced an old wooden bridge in 1948.

Old boatyard on Back Creek

A WEEK AFTER this photograph was taken, this picturesque shed, old wooden dock, and persimmon tree with its roots in salt water had vanished before a bulldozer.

"MERCY ME!" is what an oldtimer would exclaim who hadn't seen his hometown and its waters since 1950. With the decline of commercial sail, the increase of leisure-time for pleasure-boating, with quick access by car from Washington and Baltimore across the new Eastport bridge, marinas on Spa Creek and Back Creek have proliferated.

The boating trades are rediscovering and revitalizing an old industry in an old town that has always been waterminded. Whereas two centuries ago the water was alive with canoes, skiffs, wherries, sloops, barges rowed by slaves, snows and schooners, today an equal variety of craft enjoys this splendid harbor. Here is a snug and protected anchorage, a gentle climate, a shoreline free of rocks and marsh where mosquitoes and flies can breed. Fog and the tidal flow are minimal. An hour or two's run can take you across the Bay or up into a serpentine quiet creek where privacy and a sense of nature unspoiled is implicit. Repair shops and wharfage, which a century ago served only sleepy beat-up shipyards used by fishermen, now support competent boatyards and ever-expanding mooring. A central Chesapeake Bay location is further enhanced by a town with a fascinating history and beautifully preserved buildings. The presence of the Naval Academy is the frosting on the cake for the yachtsman and visitor.

Sloops tied up on Back Creek

A QUIET COVE on the south shore of Back Creek as yet undefiled. Coves like this on four creeks within Annapolis township account for the surprising length of its shoreline, eighteen and a half miles.

YACHTS moored in a yard at the front of Shipwright Street frame the Victorian spire of St. Mary's Church.

Recess at St. Mary's School

THE ANCIENT CITY AGAIN

THE PROPERTY shown here is owned by the Roman Catholic monks of the Redemptorist Order. Essentially the church and school of St. Mary's Parish, it faces Spa Creek at the south end of Duke of Gloucester Street, and Shipwright Street borders it on the west. Built in the early 1700s the house was the seat of Charles Carroll of Annapolis, who is so named to distinguish him from his father, Charles Carroll Settler or Emigrant, and from his more famous patriot son, Charles Carroll of Carrollton, The Signer.

The second Charles chose this remote corner of the early town for unusual reasons. Charles Carroll of Annapolis was a Catholic, and penal enactments against Catholics in England blighted his whole civic status in the colony. He could not vote or hold public office, practice law, hold church services or instruct the young. The wealth his father, The Settler, left him represented his only avenue to influence and prestige. So he lent money, and by his middle age had amassed the largest fortune in the Colonies. His account books show that about two-thirds of Annapolis' population, high and low, were at one time or another in his debt. Yet educated abroad, he preferred the life of a social and intellectual center, so selected a site removed from town for his homestead.

When he died in 1782, his only son, Charles Carroll of Carrollton, inherited this fortune, and at the end of the Revolution was considered the wealthiest man in America. The estate consisted of somewhere between seventy and eighty-five thousand fertile acres in Maryland, Pennsylvania and New York. In the early 1770s he had seen the handwriting on the wall, and converted a major portion of this land from tobacco into wheat, and, with 316 slaves alone on his Maryland estates in Howard and Frederick Counties, his holdings approximated £88,000. This was augmented by an indeterminate amount deriving from inherited mortgages and loans out at interest, and from those he contracted for himself. Historians have assessed all this as worth around $2,000,000. Undoubtedly nobody risked as much for the American cause in a material sense as this dedicated and generous Catholic patriot.

After the Revolution, and until he died, The Signer made his home at Doughoregan Manor near Elk Ridge, Maryland, although he always visited Annapolis for important events, staying in his birthplace, the family seat. On his death the Annapolis estate was bequeathed to four daughters who donated it in 1852 to the Redemptorists. St. Mary's Church was built in 1859 and the steeple in 1876. Founded in 1732 in Italy, the Society of the Redemptorists came to America in 1832.

CHARLES CARROLL of Carrollton, 1737-1832. This
painting by Thomas Sully hangs in the rotunda of the
State House. Maryland's Old Roman was the last of the
fifty-two Signers of the Declaration of Independence to
die.

ON SHIPWRIGHT STREET at the west corner of the Redemptorist property is the lovely old Upton Scott house which Winston Churchill had in mind as the home of his hero Richard Carvel.

Born in County Antrim, Ireland, Dr. Scott came to Annapolis in 1753 with Horatio Sharpe, Royal Governor of the Province, became his physician and built his house in 1765. During the Revolution he remained in Annapolis as a Loyalist. Perhaps his wife from Frederick County, Elizabeth Ross Key, had something to do with it. Later her grandnephew, Francis Scott Key, lived with the Scotts when a student at St. John's. Dr. Scott died in his ninety-third year, having lived sixty years in Annapolis, and is buried at St. Anne's Cemetery by the creek.

After the Redemptorists settled on the point, the Sisters of Notre Dame acquired the Scott house and recently sold it to private owners.

The Upton Scott House

The Ridout harbor front

JOHN RIDOUT was a young Oxford graduate when he came to Annapolis in 1753 with Governor Sharpe as the latter's personal secretary. He seems to have been not only brainy but personable. Both the Governor and his secretary courted Mary Ogle. But she chose the younger man, and together they planned this impressive house around 1765.

It is interesting to note how the Palladian window was handled. Since the house has no third story, the window is allowed to interrupt the main cornice so as to obtain the necessary height for the semi-circular sash. Some architects today have felt that perhaps a piece of the cornice was missing, and that the problem was not well handled. But a local architect familiar with Annapolis Georgian sees this irregularity as the result of an owner's whimsy. Perhaps the walls of the house were almost up, and the owner suddenly decided, as owners have done before and since, that he would like to have a Palladian window. Or perhaps it was the wife. In any case, the accommodation was made as handily as time and materials allowed, and the result is indeed charming.

The property retains the same dimensions as the year it was purchased over two centuries ago, and remains today in the same Ridout family.

The right-hand window of the portico is a dummy and is painted black.

The garden stoop

The Capitol dome and Market Street from across Spa Creek

FROM a high embankment on Boucher Street in Eastport, and looking across Spa Creek, the telephoto lens gives a view of old Market Street leading up its rather steep grade. In 1718 when James Stoddert drew his map, there was wharfage at its foot where the Colonials could moor and bring their produce up to the public market at the intersection of Market and Duke of Gloucester Streets.

WITH THE HOUSE Charles Carroll the Settler built we touch the early years of the Ancient City. In 1688 this Catholic son of Erin of twenty-eight years emigrated from his native Littermouna, King's County, Ireland, to St. Mary's on the Patuxent River. The hawk uprising which embellished his crest proved symbolic. Moving to Annapolis in 1694 with the General Assembly, he became Lord Baltimore's Agent, found himself in a position to buy good tobacco land, loaned out his profits at 10%, and died in 1720 worth £60,000.

While we cannot prove The Settler actually dwelt here, many records survive from which to build the history of the house. Stoddert describes the point where the public market space began as "at the north east corner of the shade of a brick house belonging to Charles Carroll esq." So the house stood in 1718 when the surveyor made his map.

In 1720 the second Charles (later called "of Annapolis") became head of the family when The Settler died.

That 139 was not regarded as a homestead seems clear from its fate. Surrounding the house was considerable property belonging to the Carrolls. Sometime before 1729 the house and yard were lifted out as a tidy piece approximating 9,400 square feet and swapped with one Thomas Larkin for an unknown parcel. Larkin sold it to the Hon. George Plater, a tobacco planter from St. Mary's County who had just married a wealthy widow. Plater was Secretary to Baltimore's Council, and he and his wife probably used it as their town house. He died in 1755, and his son George sold the property in 1762 to John Hall, an attorney, who along with George Plater, Samuel Chase, William Paca and others were patriot-lawyers in the thick of everything in revolutionary Annapolis.

After this we know little until 1852 when, dilapidated, run down and renting for only $150 a year, the house was sold at public auction to the R. R. Magruder family.

After seventy-five years in the Magruders' hands, it went from one Navy officer to a second, and finally in 1941 to Paul Mellon of Upperville, Virginia. Stripping off the inside paint, he restored its fine red pine woodwork. In 1948 he presented the house to St. John's College, where he had been a student, for a President's House. The present owner bought it from St. John's.

Presenting a sharp contrast to the imposing Georgian houses in the vicinity, 139 points up the sturdy simplicity of the dwellings built by the gentry after Annapolis became the provincial capital.

139 Market Street

THE southwest bedchamber, over the livingroom and tucked away under a steeply pitched "A" roof, looks substantially as it did in the Eighteenth Century. The element over the hearth is solid and the owner does not know why it is there.

ORIGINAL WALLBOARDS are visible in the back of the Queen Anne cupboard. Its scooped-out shelves are typical of that era and style.

Acton Place

IN 1657 Richard Acton was granted the large tract of land just outside the Old Town boundary and bordering on Spa Creek. By 1760 Philip Hammond had a tobacco plantation here, lived in this house, and shipped tobacco from his own dock on Spa Creek. Matthias Hammond who built the Hammond-Harwood House was Philip's youngest son. The hyphen and wing are considered of later date.

A PRINCE OF SERENDIP on Charles Street.

In 1745 Jonas Green of Yankee extraction began to publish the Maryland *Gazette* from this house on Charles Street. One of the earliest Colonial newspapers, the *Gazette* was first published by William Parks in 1727 and then abandoned seven years later. After three years in Philadelphia with his cousin Benjamin Franklin, Jonas Green came to Annapolis in 1738, was appointed Printer to the Province, bought this house, and in 1745 reactivated the defunct *Gazette,* imitating the *Spectator* and the *Rambler* published in London. Suspended during 1777-1779, publication continued from this house until 1839 when the grandson of the original Jonas died and the *Gazette* was sold. In its 240th year under the same name, the *Gazette* is still published today as a weekly in Glen Burnie, Maryland.

While its origin is still cloudy, this is considered one of the oldest houses in the Ancient City and is still in the hands of Green family descendants.

An early issue of the Maryland Gazette

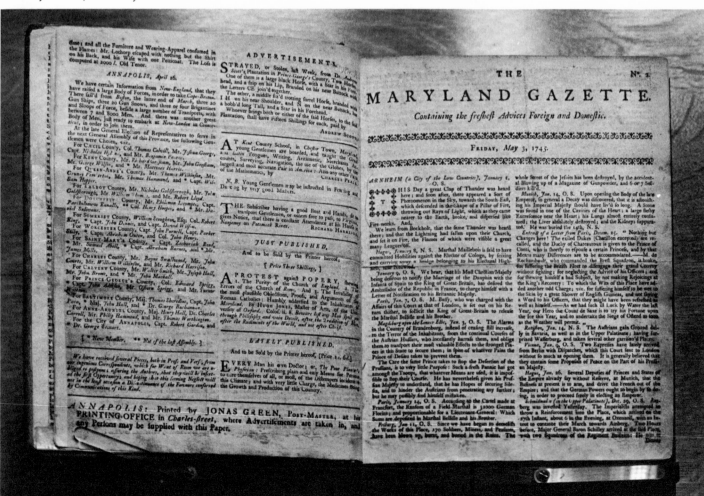

The Jonas Green House

Looking up Duke of Gloucester Street to St. Anne's

RUNNING FROM the Circle to Spa Creek, this principal thoroughfare was named for the little Duke of Gloucester, the only one of Queen Anne's seventeen children to live until he was ten.

THE MARYLAND INN building which dates from the 1770s is prominently situated at Church Circle on the pie-shaped lot laid out for the use of the Drummer of the Town, or the Town Crier, about 1696. Always an historic lot, its chain of title includes many distinguished Maryland family names like Chew, Lloyd, Dulany, Paca, Dorsey, Bordley, Hyde, Bowie and others.

In 1772 Thomas Hyde of Severn acquired a long-term leasehold on the lot and proceeded to build the front portion. It was described in old records as an "Inn". Hyde advertised it in the *Gazette* January 31, 1782, and September 10, 1789, as an "Elegant brick house adjoining Church Circle, 100 feet front, 3 story high, 22 rooms, 20 fireplaces, 2 kitchens . . One of the first houses in the State for a house of entertainment, for which purpose it was originally intended." It was known as the *King of France Tavern*.

The Maryland Hotel Company incorporated in 1868 acquired the property, held it for a long time, and undoubtedly added the mansard and Victorian trim typical of the post-bellum era.